DATE DUE

OC 1 '98			
OC 23 '98			
DE 27 '98			
DE 8K '98			
NO 3 '98			
NO 9 '98			
DE 1 '98			
DE 9 '98			
DE 17 '98			
JA 8 '99			
JA 6 '99			
MR 18 '99			
FE 23 '00			
MR 7 '00			
MR 15 '00			

Demco, Inc. 38-293

America's Game
Colorado Rockies

Bob Italia

ABDO & Daughters
PUBLISHING

Published by Abdo & Daughters, 4940 Viking Dr., Suite 622, Edina, MN 55435.

Cover photo: Allsport
Interior photos: Wide World Photo, pages 7, 10, 13, 17, 21, 23, 25.
Allsport, pages 1, 5, 15, 28.

Edited by Paul Joseph

Library of Congress Cataloging–in–Publication Data

Italia, Bob, 1955-
    Colorado Rockies / Bob Italia
        p. cm. — (America's game)
    Includes index.
    Summary: A history of the team that brought major league baseball to the mountain regions of America.
    ISBN   1-56239-682-X
    1. Colorado Rockies (Baseball team)—Juvenile literature.
[1. Colorado Rockies (Baseball team)—History. 2. Baseball—History.]   I. Title. II. Series.
GV875.C78I83   1997
796.357' 64' 0978883—dc20   96-25154
                                                                   CIP
                                                                   AC

Contents

Colorado Rockies

When the Colorado Rockies entered the National League in 1993, they brought Major League Baseball to the mountain regions of America. Since that time, the Rockies' success on and off the field has been amazing.

In its first year, the team sold more than 24,000 season tickets before it even took the field. Then Colorado drew a record one million fans in their first 17 home appearances. On Opening Day 1993 in Denver, over 80,000 fans packed Mile High Stadium to cheer their new team.

Bringing the team to Denver was not easy. It took the efforts of the region's politicians, business leaders, and baseball fans—including the wealthy Coors family of brewing fame. The Rockies drew fans in record numbers—and made the playoffs in only their third year.

Sluggers Andres Galarraga, Larry Walker, and Dante Bichette have made the Rockies' lineup one of the most potent in the National League. Once Colorado solves its pitching woes, they should find themselves in the hunt for a World Series title.

Facing page: The Rockies' Andres Galarraga steps to the plate.

Once Upon A Time. . .

The Rockies owe their existence to businessman Bob Howsam. Shortly after World War II, Howsam bought a minor league team called the Denver Bears. Denver already had enjoyed a relationship with professional baseball. Pro games had been played in the region as early as the 1880s. But those teams did not survive.

In 1948, Howsam felt the time was right for a permanent baseball team in Denver. He raised enough money for a new stadium and moved his team. The following year, the Bears set a minor league attendance record.

Howsam enjoyed success into the 1950s. But then televised baseball games began to cut into attendance. Fewer and fewer fans went to Bears games despite the exciting play of Marv Throneberry and Whitey Herzog.

Howsam knew that it was time to get into the major leagues. But he took it one step further. In 1959, Howsam teamed with baseball executive Branch Rickey and potential owners in Houston and Buffalo to form the Continental League. It had teams in Denver, Houston, Minneapolis-St. Paul, New York, Toronto, Atlanta, Buffalo, and Dallas-Fort Worth. Rickey was the league commissioner.

Taking notice of the new league, the established major league teams announced they would begin expanding in 1960. That expansion brought teams to Minneapolis, Los Angeles, Houston, and New York. Facing increased competition, Howsam and his new league suffered financial losses. He was forced to sell the Bears to Denver businessman Gerald Phipps.

Howsam moved from Denver and worked as general manager for the St. Louis Cardinals and the Cincinnati Reds. But his work with the Continental League would one day help Denver's attempt at an expansion team in the 1990s.

In the late 1960s and early 1970s, Bears Stadium expanded to hold the 76,000 fans for the Broncos football team. The city of Denver bought the stadium in 1968 and renamed it Mile High Stadium.

During that time, the Bears still drew fans. The major league expansion in 1969 passed over Denver because no one in the city wanted to pay the high cost of starting a franchise.

An aerial view of Bears Stadium in 1954.

More Attempts

In the mid-1970s, billionaire oil man Marvin Davis of Denver made several attempts to purchase an existing major league team. He offered bids for the Chicago White Sox in 1976 and the Baltimore Orioles in 1977. When those deals fell through, he spent years trying to buy the Athletics. But that deal finally ended in the mid-1980s. By that time, Denver's economy was not doing well. But interest in Major League Baseball was strong again. Mayor Federico Peña concluded that Major League Baseball would help pump millions of dollars into the local economy each year. So, he created the Denver Baseball Commission (DBC) to help bring a major league team to the city.

In 1984, the DBC invited the two league presidents and a dozen baseball executives to Denver for a tour and a party. A Bears baseball game attracted 32,926 fans at Mile High Stadium. But the Commission's efforts did not bring Major League Baseball to Denver. The league did not plan to expand anytime soon.

To get Major League Baseball in Denver, an even greater effort was needed. In the late 1980s, the Colorado Baseball Commission was formed to lobby baseball's owners. Then Colorado Senator Tim Wirth started the Senate Task Force on the Expansion of Major League Baseball. Momentum for expansion was growing.

But baseball commissioner Peter Ueberroth wasn't budging on the issue. It took much more political pressure before the league entertained expansion ideas once again. Baseball's owners decided they did not want to anger the U.S. Senate. On June 14, 1990, the National League released a schedule for a two-team expansion by the 1993 season.

With the Mile High City's skyline as a backdrop, Coors Field opened in Denver in 1995.

Putting On A Show

The league owners wanted prospective cities to provide a first-class stadium for baseball. To raise the money, Colorado politicians looked to the taxpayers for help. They asked for a small increase in the sales tax to raise funds for a new stadium.

The tax increase was voted upon on August 14, 1990. It was approved by 54 percent of the voters. In 1992, ground was broken on the new stadium to be called Coors Field. Before its completion, the new baseball team would play at Mile High Stadium. Denver had support for a new stadium. Now the city needed support for the team.

Denver lawyer Paul Jacobs was put in charge of finding investors willing to pay the $95 million franchise fee—plus another $20 to $30 million to start up the team. In 1990, with just days remaining before the league's deadline, a large ownership group was finally formed.

The National League Expansion Committee chose six major cities as possible franchise sites. Then the committee visited each location to examine the baseball stadiums and fan support. On March 26, 1991, the committee arrived in Denver. City officials were ready.

At Mile High Stadium, the electronic scoreboard showed a game in progress. At the site of the future Coors Field, a sandlot game was in process, featuring local Little Leaguers. In downtown Denver, over 3,000 fans chanted "BASEBALL! BASEBALL! BASEBALL!" The committee members were impressed.

The display of fan support, the plans for a new stadium, and Denver's attempt to establish the Continental League experiment all stood in the city's favor.

A Franchise At Last

On June 10, 1991, the Expansion Committee picked Denver and South Florida as the sites for the two expansion teams. The major league owners approved the choices on July 5, 1991. Denver finally had a major league team. That same day, the Colorado Baseball Partnership announced that the new team would be called the Rockies. Their logo would be a baseball set on top of purple mountains.

The ownership group named Bob Gebhard, a former vice president of the Minnesota Twins, as general manager. In 1992, Gebhard scouted all 26 major league clubs in preparation for the November expansion draft.

Don Baylor was chosen as the Rockies first-ever manager. Baylor was an 18-year American League veteran. Even more, he had played in three World Series, including 1987 when he batted .385 in five games for the victorious Minnesota Twins.

Baylor had never managed in the majors before he came to the Rockies. For his coaching staff, he chose pitching coach Larry Bearnarth, first base coach Ron Hassey, batting coach Amos Otis, and third base coach Jerry Royster. Former manager Don Zimmer also joined the team as bench coach.

Don Baylor answers questions at a press conference after being named the first manager of the Colorado Rockies in 1992.

Building The Team

In 1992, the Rockies started a minor league team at Bend, Oregon. Fifty players were selected in the June 1992 Free Agent Draft. Forty signed with the team and reported to the minor leagues. The Rockies' first-ever first-round draft pick was pitcher John Burke from the University of Florida.

Throughout the summer, Gebhard and his staff prepared for the Expansion Draft, which would allow the Rockies to select unprotected players from each of the existing major league teams. For the first time in history, the expansion teams could choose players from both the National and American leagues.

The draft was held on November 17, 1992. The Rockies won the first pick and chose Atlanta pitcher David Nied. The draft lasted for hours. Fans cheered every selection. Top Rockies' draft picks included Yankee third baseman Charlie Hayes, Brewers' pitcher Darren Holmes, Padres' outfielder Jerald Clark, Texas outfielder Kevin Reimer, Los Angeles infielder Eric Young, and Boston infielder Jody Reed. The Rockies immediately traded Reimer to Milwaukee for outfielder Dante Bichette, then sent Reed to Los Angeles for pitcher Rudy Seanez. Free agents Daryl Boston, Andres Galarraga, and Jeff Parrett joined the team during the winter of 1992-93.

Facing page: Dante Bichette batting in a game against the Chicago Cubs.

Play Ball!

The Rockies opened the 1993 baseball season on April 5 at Shea Stadium, where they lost to the New York Mets 3-0. Four days later came the home opener in Denver. Over 80,000 fans packed Mile High Stadium. The attendance set a major league record for a regular season game. The Rockies did not disappoint their fans, winning 11-4 over the Montreal Expos.

The Rockies' first season was a complete success. The team set a record for victories by an expansion club with 67. They also drew nearly 4.5 million fans to Mile High Stadium—the most ever by a major league team.

Andres Galarraga was the biggest star. He led the National League with a .370 batting average, becoming the first player from a first-year expansion club to win a batting crown. Dante Bichette and Charlie Hayes also had outstanding seasons. The Rockies' bullpen, which got off to a shaky start, became one of the team's strong points.

Facing page: The Rockies' first baseman Adres Galarraga slams a two-run homer against the Chicago Cubs.

Colorado

Don Baylor won the NL Manager of the Year Award in 1995.

In 1993, Andres Galarraga led the National League with a .370 batting average, becoming the first player from a first-year expansion club to win a batting crown.

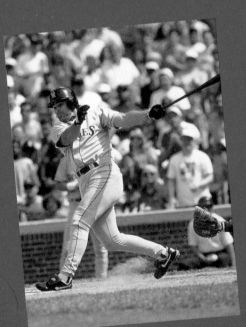

In 1995, Dante Bichette hit .340, with a league-leading 40 HRs and 128 RBIs.

Rockies

In the 1994 season, pitcher Marvin Freeman posted a 10-2 record, with a 2.8 ERA.

In 1995, Larry Walker came away with 36 HRs, 101 RBIs, a .306 average, and a .607 slugging percentage.

In 1995, Vinny Castilla batted .309, with 32 HRs and 90 RBIs.

The 1994 Season

In 1994, Galarraga was in the midst of another fine season when a pitch broke his hand on July 28. Despite their 50-54 record, the Rockies were in second place in the NL West, just a half game out of first. But then the season ended abruptly two weeks later because of a players' strike. By then, the Rockies had slipped to third, 6.5 games out. Still, their 53-64 record was impressive for a second-year team. Even more impressive was their 28-31 road record.

Galarraga finished the season with outstanding numbers. His 31 home runs led the team, and was fifth-best in the National League. He also knocked in 85 runs and batted .319. Dante Bichette blasted 27 home runs and drove in a team-high 95 runs. His .304 batting average was fifth-best on the team.

There were many more hitting stars on the 1994 Colorado Rockies. Mike Kingery led the way with an outstanding .349 batting average. Vinny Castilla was second with a .331 mark, and Ellis Burks batted .322.

But the pitching still needed improvement, despite the efforts of Marvin Freeman, who posted a 10-2 record with a 2.80 earned run average (ERA). David Nied had a 9-7 mark and a disappointing 4.80 ERA. Kevin Ritz (5-6) was the only other starter with five or more wins. Closer Bruce Ruffin recorded a team-high 16 saves.

Pitcher Marvin Freeman

The 1995 Season

During the off-season, Gebhard made left-handed hitting free agent Larry Walker his top priority. Gebhard was successful in signing the slugger, who would bat between Bichette and Galarraga.

In 1995, the Rockies moved into beautiful new Coors Field, drawing 3.3 million fans. Baylor won NL Manager of the Year honors as Colorado finished 77-67—just one game behind Los Angeles in the NL West. Even more, the Rockies proved to be tough at home, posting a 44-28 mark. Their outstanding efforts earned them a wild card playoff berth.

The Walker acquisition proved to be a success. He and third baseman Castilla joined Bichette and Galarraga as only the second quartet of teammates ever to lash at least 30 home runs each in a season. The single-best performance came from Bichette, who hit .340 with a league-leading 40 homers and 128 RBIs. Other key Rockies were Galarraga (31 HR, 106 RBI), Vinny Castilla (32 HR, 90 RBI, .309), Eric Young (.317 and an NL-leading 9 triples), and Larry Walker (36 HR, 101 RBI, .306 and second in the NL with a .607 slugging percentage). John VanderWal led the team with a .347 average. As a team, the Rockies batted .282—tops in the National League. Their 200 home runs were also a league best.

Facing page: Larry Walker connects against the St. Louis Cardinals.

But for all the bashing and solid bullpen performances, the starting pitching cost the Rockies the Western Division lead in the closing week of the season—and even came close to losing their wild card berth. Only a comeback from an 8-2 deficit against the San Francisco Giants on the last day of the season headed off a winner-take-all, one-game playoff with the Houston Astros.

Bill Swift was the only reliable starter as he posted a 9-3 record. But his 4.94 ERA was disappointing. Bret Saberhagen's 7-6 record was also disappointing, as was his 4.18 ERA.

Vinny Castilla watches his two-run homer take flight in a game against the San Diego Padres.

The Playoffs

Still, the Rockies—in only their third year—had made the playoffs. And as impossible as it seemed, they had a chance to reach—and win—the World Series. To get there, they had to defeat the pitching-rich Atlanta Braves.

The best-of-five division series against the Atlanta Braves began in Colorado. But the home field advantage the Rockies enjoyed most of the year failed them when they needed it the most. In Game 1, the Braves took a 5-4 lead heading into the bottom of the ninth inning. The Rockies loaded the bases, but were forced to use a pitcher to pinch-hit in their final at-bat. They failed to score.

In Game 2, the little-used Mike Mordecai knocked in the go-ahead run with a two-out single in the ninth inning, helping rally the Braves past the Rockies 7-4 and sending Atlanta home with a 2-0 lead in their NL playoff series. Fred McGriff's RBI single had tied the score in the ninth. The Rockies compounded their troubles by making an error that brought in two more runs.

Larry Walker's three-run homer off Glavine and Andres Galarraga's RBI single off Alejandro Peña had given Colorado a 4-3 lead going to the ninth. But Chipper Jones led off the ninth by slicing a double down the left-field line off Curtis Leskanic.

Mike Munoz then gave up a bloop single to McGriff, which scored Jones. David Justice flied out, and Darren Holmes struck out Javy Lopez. Mike Devereaux then singled to center, with McGriff taking second. Then Mordecai lined a single to center to drive home the go-ahead run.

Mordecai took second on the throw home. Rafael Belliard then hit a routine grounder to second, but Eric Young's throw to first was low and wide, letting in two more runs.

It was the second-straight blown save for the Rockies in as many games. Leskanic gave up Jones' winning homer in the ninth in Game 1. The Rockies had 15 blown saves during the season.

"The disheartening thing is we should be 2-0 going to Atlanta," Rockies manager Baylor said. "We kind of gave in to Mordecai at 3-0. Wc've beaten ourselves the last three years against the Braves. It seems like every time we kick a ball, they come back to beat us."

Now Colorado had to win the next three games if they wanted to keep their World Series hopes alive.

With the series switching to Atlanta, the Rockies surprised the Braves with a dramatic 7-5, 10-inning win. After squandering a late-inning lead for the third-straight game, the Rockies rallied for the victory.

On the strength of two-run homers from Eric Young and Castilla, Colorado took 3-0 and 5-3 leads. They had the Braves down in the ninth inning with a 5-4 lead, two outs and an 0-2 count on pinch-hitter Luis Polonia. But Polonia blooped an opposite-field single to bring home the tying run.

In the top of the 10th inning, Bichette got his third hit of the game. That eventually led to an intentional walk to Larry Walker, setting up dramatic RBI singles by Galarraga and Castilla that iced the game. The Rockies were still alive. One more win and the series would be tied.

However, the Braves ended the Rockies' World Series dreams in Game 4 behind consecutive homers and five RBIs by Fred McGriff and a 5-for-5 performance by Marquis Grissom. Atlanta took the series three games to one.

For the second-straight game, the Rockies went ahead 3-0, this time on Bichette's three-run homer in the top of the third. The Braves overcame that in the bottom of the inning against Bret Saberhagen. Four-straight hits after two were out with nobody on base—including a two-run double by Chipper Jones and a two-run homer by McGriff—put the Braves ahead 4-3. The Braves added their final three runs similarly, with McGriff singling home the last two.

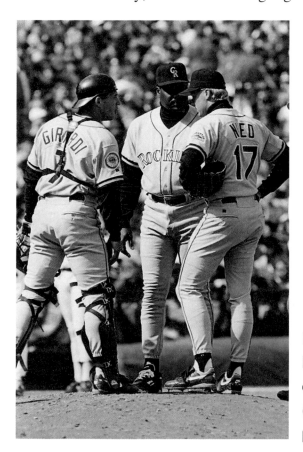

Rockies' manager Don Baylor is flanked by catcher Joe Girardi (left) and starting pitcher David Nied.

Future Champions

Though the Rockies' season ended in disappointment, the future looks bright. The lineup is loaded with hitters who can change the course of a game with one swing of the bat. If management can secure a solid pitching staff, Colorado fans may soon be singing the praises of a world championship team.

Larry Walker smacks a hit during a game against the San Diego Padres.

Glossary

All-Star: A player who is voted by fans as the best player at one position in a given year.

American League (AL): An association of baseball teams formed in 1900 which make up one-half of the major leagues.

American League Championship Series (ALCS): A best-of-seven-game playoff with the winner going to the World Series to face the National League Champions.

Batting Average: A baseball statistic calculated by dividing a batter's hits by the number of times at bat.

Earned Run Average (ERA): A baseball statistic which calculates the average number of runs a pitcher gives up per nine innings of work.

Fielding Average: A baseball statistic which calculates a fielder's success rate based on the number of chances the player has to record an out.

Hall of Fame: A memorial for the greatest baseball players of all time, located in Cooperstown, New York.

Home Run (HR): A play in baseball where a batter hits the ball over the outfield fence scoring everyone on base as well as the batter.

Major Leagues: The highest ranking associations of professional baseball teams in the world, currently consisting of the American and National Baseball Leagues.

Minor Leagues: A system of professional baseball leagues at levels below Major League Baseball.

National League (NL): An association of baseball teams formed in 1876 which make up one-half of the major leagues.

National League Championship Series (NLCS): A best-of-seven-game playoff with the winner going to the World Series to face the American League Champions.

Pennant: A flag which symbolizes the championship of a professional baseball league.

Pitcher: The player on a baseball team who throws the ball for the batter to hit. The pitcher stands on a mound and pitches the ball toward the strike zone area above the plate.

Plate: The place on a baseball field where a player stands to bat. It is used to determine the width of the strike zone. Forming the point of the diamond-shaped field, it is the final goal a base runner must reach to score a run.

RBI: A baseball statistic standing for *runs batted in.* Players receive an RBI for each run that scores on their hits.

Rookie: A first-year player, especially in a professional sport.

Slugging Percentage: A statistic which points out a player's ability to hit for extra bases by taking the number of total bases hit and dividing it by the number of at bats.

Stolen Base: A play in baseball when a base runner advances to the next base while the pitcher is delivering the pitch.

Strikeout: A play in baseball when a batter is called out for failing to put the ball in play after the pitcher has delivered three strikes.

Triple Crown: A rare accomplishment when a single player finishes a season leading their league in batting average, home runs, and RBIs. A pitcher can win a Triple Crown by leading the league in wins, ERA, and strikeouts.

Walk: A play in baseball when a batter receives four pitches out of the strike zone and is allowed to go to first base.

World Series: The championship of Major League Baseball played since 1903 between the pennant winners from the American and National Leagues.

Index